Preacher Named EMMA

George W. Rice

Like a tree planted by streams of water.
PSALM 1:3

Beacon Hill Press of Kansas City
Kansas City, Missouri

A
Preacher
Named
EMMA

Emma B. Irick

To every woman of every generation
with courage and faithfulness
to fulfill God's call to preach
the gospel of Jesus Christ

Contents

A
Preacher
Named
EMMA

1
Healthy Family Roots

It was no accident that Emma Wyland Irick became one of the outstanding lady preachers in the entire history of the Holiness Movement. Her family modeled and instilled into her young life the principles expressed in Psalm 1. Her own dying out to sin and her teenage commitment to follow God's will at any cost qualified her to become "like a tree planted by streams of [living] water" (v. 3). To her final earthly day she found "delight . . . in the law of the LORD" (v. 2) and yielded her "fruit in season" (v. 3). She exemplified God's promise that "blessed is the man" (v. 1) (or the woman) who trusts his or her life and career to "the LORD [who] watches over the way of the righteous" (v. 6).

Emma Wyland was born January 24, 1888, on a Jewell County farm in north central Kansas. She was the second of five children born to William and Ella Wyland. These devout parents had inherited their God-loving and churchgoing habits from their own parents. One of Emma's first childhood memories was of when her Grandfather Wyland was dying. As she later described it, he "laid his big hand on my forehead and prayed that God would make me a blessing." Her grandfather's covenant prayer was always a treasured memory to Emma.

Emma's father assigned regular chores to every child, to "keep them out of meanness." Therefore she never played house, as most children do, but began early to *keep* house. Her mother was almost an invalid, so Emma had unusually heavy home responsibilities. At the age of 7 she was cooking breakfast, and by 10 years of age she was sewing her own clothes and baking bread for the family.

In season, Emma also helped with outdoor farm chores, including all the planting, cultivating, and harvesting tasks of that Midwestern farm-ranch. This habit of hard work helped develop her strong constitution and positive attitude toward life. Emma never resented these hardworking demands of her rural family. For the rest of her life, she tackled her studies and teaching, along with the varied demands of her preaching and homemaking chores, with the same happy energy she had demonstrated as a growing child and teenager. She grew up with the philosophy that the only task one should be ashamed of was a job done poorly.

Emma treasured her close-knit and very happy homelife. She considered her greatest heritage to be the family altar, where she first learned to pray. Her first definite answer to prayer was the result of a near-fatal attack her mother had suffered, when the doctor despaired of her life. Seven-year-old Emma, brokenhearted, went to the orchard to pray under the old peach tree. She begged God to let her mother live because her baby sister, Eva, really needed her.

God gave Emma assurance that her mother would not die at this time, and Emma reassured the anxious adults that the Lord had told her so. This definite answer to prayer became a lifetime bulwark to her faith. She described the experience nearly 80 years later: "Whenever Satan 'comes in like a flood,' I point him to the peach tree where God answered my childhood prayer."[1]

Emma was fascinated by what her older brother, Ray, was learning in school. Her mother arranged for Emma to enter first grade at the Sweet Home country school at the tender age of 4. Basic to all her training, she developed a love of reading that became the foundation of not only her education but also her lifetime passion for knowledge and effectiveness.

After completing her local grade school studies, Emma attended high school in Jewell, Kansas, eight miles from her farm home. She drove her own buggy, drawn by her little black horse, Cricket. Thanks to her early start, she was able to graduate at only 16 years of age.

During her junior year of high school, Emma accepted Christ as her Savior. It was on October 23, 1902, during a revival at her parents' Methodist church. Through that experience she developed a conviction that a local church could increase its impact if more attention were given to the spiritual needs of children. She developed this focus further when she later became an evangelist and a pastor in her own right.

Emma always gave special attention to children and youth, feeling strongly that God's plan was to save them early in life. She believed this would help them avoid the eventual gross effects of sin as well as establish attitudes and habits essential to a lifetime of spiritual victory and effective Christian service.

2

Growing and Branching Out

Emma enjoyed "wonderful teachers and a very godly superintendent of schools."[1] These influential individuals were always interested in Emma's future ambitions and goals. They encouraged her to set her goals high and go on for further training—in an era when this was not the pattern for most young people.

When Emma graduated from high school in 1904, she was challenged to enroll at Northwest Teachers College in Alva, Oklahoma. During that summer she took care of her regular household chores, as well as the extra outdoor work that was a part of her farm-ranch home. She also cut and hauled firewood to earn money for new shoes to wear to college and for the train fare to get her there. The rest of her wardrobe consisted of hand-me-down clothes from a cousin.

Emma's family was financially unable to help her with any of her school expenses. They always encouraged her that God would supply her needs if she would totally trust Him. Emma marveled that they trusted her to leave home for college with absolutely no money—and she had no acquaintances at the school of her choice.

God did not fail this 16-year-old girl. On the train she providentially met a girl returning for her senior year at Northwest Teachers College. This new friend took Emma to the boarding house where she lived. There Emma made an agreement to work for her room and board. She began by cooking supper Saturday night after she arrived in Alva. On Sunday she went to church. She arose at 4 A.M. Monday morning, "put out a big wash, fixed breakfast, and was at the college at eight o'clock to register for classes."[2]

It was not easy to attend school and work at the same time, but Emma was determined to receive her education. Early in her second year she passed her teacher's examination and was licensed to teach school. She left immediately to teach at a one-room country school in Homestead, Oklahoma, where she taught 46 pupils in seven grades. She finished her college work by attending summer school during the next two years of teaching. She was able to open class each day with Bible reading and prayer, and she later rejoiced that three of her pupils entered the ministry in the years ahead. Even before she received God's definite call to become a preacher of His gospel, she was doing "the work of an evangelist" (2 Tim. 4:5).

Meanwhile, things were not going well at her home in Kansas. Drought, reverses, and low prices finally forced Emma's father to sell out. During her freshman year the family moved to a farm in Major County, just west of Enid, Oklahoma, and not far from Alva, where their daughter was in school.

The family's move to Oklahoma proved to be a blessing to the entire Wyland family. Here her father for the first time heard the message of Bible holiness. Emma arrived home just in time to witness her father seeking God at the church altar for His second blessing. Because of the example he had consistently reflected, Emma realized that his initial religious experience was still good. "No one could pray as he did around the family altar and not have true salvation,"[3] she said. That night, as Mr. Wyland put everything on God's altar, Emma heard him cry out, "Lord, it's Yours, everything: family, home, time, talent, all I have, all I am."[4] As she later testified, "Then the fire fell, and he began to praise the Lord." She thought to herself, "If my father needs heart holiness, then I need it too,"[5] and her heart became hungry for this wonderful experience of God's sanctifying grace.

Wanting everyone else to experience the reality of what he had found, Emma's father sent to Kansas for a Holiness revival team he had heard about. He guaranteed to meet their expenses if they would come to his community. They came and stayed in the Wyland home, sleeping in the children's rooms. The boys slept in the barn and Emma in the smokehouse. (She was always grateful that this was the closest she ever got to smoking.)

On February 11, 1905, the evangelist's message was on Heb. 12:1. The Word came alive to Emma: "Lay aside every weight, and the sin which doth so easily beset us" (KJV). As she later declared, "That first sermon on second blessing holiness met the soul hunger that I knew I had need of long before I had heard of the remedy for inward sin."[6]

For three days and nights Emma fasted and prayed until she felt she had put everything on God's altar. But she could not find His definite witness that His promised work of grace was really accomplished. On a bitterly cold Saturday, she insisted that she should travel to a cottage prayer meeting scheduled for that afternoon.

She arrived at the little log home as the group was singing "Singing I go along life's road." Placing herself behind the stove, she purposed, "I'll stay here until I get sanctified or wear my knees out."[7] One by one, she reviewed all the areas of her consecration and put everything on God's altar.

That was a costly choice for this 17-year-old student. She had been teaching a Sunday School class, but a leader in the group told her that the class no longer wanted her as their teacher if she was interested in this new holiness blessing. Emma's answer was emphatic: "If I never teach another Sunday School class, I want this experience above everything else in the world."[8]

In later years Emma testified, "The Lord spoke to me, 'I not only want what you have. I want you! I want you to preach My gospel.' I replied emphatically, 'I don't want to!' Immediately I was in trouble. My ambition for many years had been to be a medical doctor. Then the Lord said, 'You preach, and I will give you workers, preachers, missionaries, and doctors. I will be with you always: I will never leave you or forsake you.'"[9] In that hour, Emma answered His call to be a preacher instead of the doctor she had dreamed of becoming. She often declared in later years that she never regretted her decision.

Furthermore, Emma had already become engaged to a well-to-do young farmer and dairyman. Now she recognized that he was lacking in spiritual grounding and total commitment. So she told him that she could not marry him, thus breaking the engagement. This was another decision she never regretted. The matter was settled. She would be God's lady preacher—even a single lady preacher, if that was His will for her.

Later, Emma chided those who claimed they had to give up so much in order to follow a Holiness lifestyle: "I always figured that when you really got holiness, you got so much that nothing else mattered. Holiness elevates, refines, and satisfies in this present life, and also gets you ready for the next world."[10]

At the end of that revival, all five Wyland children, along with their parents, left their established church home and became the nucleus of a new Wesleyan Methodist Church. All the older Wyland children professed God's call to Christian work. What an investment on the part of this Spirit-filled father!

Emma felt that a call to preach was a call to prepare. She had heard about Texas Holiness University, which had recently opened in Peniel, Texas, near what is now the city of Greenville. This new college was sponsored by the Texas Holiness Association, an interdenominational group of believers from many backgrounds, drawn together by their common love for the doctrine of Bible holiness. Emma saved her schoolteaching salary for the next two years so that she could enroll at the Bible school. This decision proved to be a vital part of God's continuing direction for her life and ministry.

3

Pruning and Preparing

When Emma Wyland answered "Yes" to God's call to preach His gospel, she hardly realized what this divine commission would mean in her life. She knew many churches had traditional prejudices against allowing any woman to preach but observed that this was not the case with the Holiness people—even though among them were some from denominational backgrounds that excluded women from the preaching ministry. The inclinations toward her original goal no doubt stemmed from the fact that her cousin was already a medical doctor. Emma realized that as a doctor she might become a useful missionary on any of several world fields, especially in India. Had God not pruned this ambition to become a female doctor, however, she may have encountered some of the same prejudices.

Emma was once challenged to preach on the subject "What the Bible Says About Women Preachers." She refused the challenge, saying, "The proof of the pudding is in the eating."[1] She knew that God had definitely called her. He blessed her efforts and opened doors for her ministry. She never felt called to defend the gospel—just to proclaim it. In the same way, she refused to defend her right to be a woman preacher but instead allowed the fruit of her ministry to speak for itself.

Once her lifetime calling was settled, Emma never deviated from this great commission. She did not wait until her education was complete to begin to exercise her gift and her challenge. Neither did she wait for church leaders to give her preferential treatment as a female preacher. Following her experience of entire sanctification, and especially in her year at Texas Holiness University, she responded to every opportunity to speak—in jails, in schools, on street corners, and in house prayer meetings. Her advice to her contemporaries who realized God's call to preach was to "keep His fire burning in your heart, prepare yourselves, and then enter every open door, trusting God for the results."[2]

Emma eventually became a powerful speaker. Her major concern was always to move her hearers to act on God's truth as it was impressed upon her mind and heart for each preaching occasion. As she later testified, "The Lord enabled me to help people get saved and sanctified, and to really live the sanctified life."[3] Her crystal-clear experiences when God had definitely saved and entirely sanctified her challenged her to guide others into the same source of holy living.

Emma's deep voice was forceful, yet she was very much a lady in appearance and demeanor. She refused to resort to mere sentimentality and storytelling as the foundation of her messages but rather drew her illustrations from her own life and ministry only as a means of illuminating some biblical truth. Emma trusted the well-presented Word to draw her hearers to Christ.

Being very homiletically minded, she built her sermons around words and ideas that would stick in the minds and hearts of her hearers. For instance, as one young boy sat under her preaching during a revival tour at his church, he heard the first of two clearly defined and well-illustrated points to her sermon "God Hates Sin." Before Emma exposited much further, the boy felt he was doomed. But she finished her message with the assurance that God loves sinners. That boy was so powerfully influenced that not only was he among those who found victory at the altar that night, but also he later became a preacher himself.

Emma was always an evangelistic preacher, whether serving as revivalist or as pastor. She was not satisfied just to deliver a message—she preached for a verdict now! This was especially true when she was exhorting on her favorite subject: second-blessing holiness. She never neglected the need for growth in grace, but she believed and preached strongly that believers could and should be sanctified entirely by God's grace and then go on to live a life of victory.

4

Cultivating a Lifetime Love

Life in Peniel at Texas Holiness University was mentally and spiritually challenging for Emma as a young teacher-preacher. She enrolled in a heavy load of courses in Bible, theology, and sermon building, along with the regular required subjects. She sat under the teaching of Dr. and Mrs. E. P. Ellyson, Professor Whitehurst, and Rev. L. B. Williams. Another strong influence on Emma was "Uncle Bud" Robinson. Since this well-known evangelist and his wife, Sally, lived in Peniel, they enjoyed entertaining many of the students in their home.

With an arrangement similar to that at the teachers college in Oklahoma, Emma worked for her room and board. An attack of typhoid fever complicated her schedule, but she made up the studies she had missed and caught up with her class. Texora Nash, her history teacher at the Holiness university, challenged her never to give up, declaring that "you have to have bulldog tenacity and determination to make your goals in life."[1]

Although Emma was prepared to serve God as a single person, that was not His plan for this beautiful and talented young lady. She enjoyed her social life and even became the special friend of a classmate, Rev. H. B. Wallin, who went on to become a well-known minister in his own right.

Not until the very night she was first licensed to preach did Emma meet her future husband. November 16, 1907, was a momentous day in the life of this young teacher starting on her new career. Mrs. Ellyson, wife of the college president, was especially anxious for her prize lady student to be officially licensed to preach. She arranged for Emma to be appointed as a delegate from Texas Holiness University to the Texas Holiness Association's annual meeting in Arlington. With Mrs. Ellyson at her side, the timid girl passed her ordeal before the Board of Examiners and was formally licensed as a preacher of the gospel.

That night all the newly licensed preachers were seated on the platform along with several returning missionaries and missionary candidates. Emma was placed next to Allie Irick, who was already a veteran evangelist. The two shared a songbook. Allie had just returned from a one-year missionary evangelistic tour with Dr. W. B. Godbey.

Each newly licensed preacher was asked to share a testimony, and when Emma spoke, Allie became interested. He asked if he could see her to her lodging place, and since H. B. Wallin had not bothered with any such invitation, though he too was among that platform group, Emma accepted. It was love at first sight for Allie, and Emma was impressed to take a second look.

Dr. E. P. Ellyson, president of the school, invited Allie to return with his group for a week of missionary services at Peniel. Allie paid Emma "all the attention the school rules would allow,"[2] and then went on to his schedule of local church revivals. During the next seven months he wrote 145 letters to

Emma and visited her 45 times (after securing the necessary permission from President Ellyson to do so, of course). Emma later described him as a very ardent admirer. Allie's whirlwind courtship persuaded Emma that he was indeed God's choice for her mate.

Although Allie was typically a female nomenclature, he had been given his name when his mother (also named Allie) died giving birth to him. Under the revival preaching of Oscar and Nettie Hudson, Allie and his brother, Solomon, were soundly converted. They both felt a call to preach and went forward that same night to be entirely sanctified. Allie became a lifetime evangelist, preaching an average of 20 revivals annually for the next 35 years. He rejoiced to see more than 1,000 people each year find Christ under his ministry.

On June 16, 1908, Emma and Allie were married in her father's home by the local Methodist minister in Ringwood, Oklahoma. Emma's father overheard the plans of youthful friends to come to their home and shivaree the newlyweds, a popular custom in that time. Mr. Wyland helped to turn these plans into an evangelism opportunity. He ordered 20 gallons of ice cream, and Emma baked 7 two-tiered cakes for the occasion. That night when the mischief-makers crowded onto the front porch, Emma's father invited them inside. Instead of the planned blank shooting and bell ringing, Allie led them in singing hymns and reading the Bible, and Emma brought an inspired gospel message. On the following day, the new couple left for a wedding trip revival near Marlow, Oklahoma.

Emma's preaching career was undoubtedly given a timely impetus when she became partners with this already established evangelist. They alternated speaking assignments, blending their unique individual preaching talents to make a powerful evangelistic team, mightily used of God in serving their generation.

God gave this couple three children: Ray, Paul, and Ruth. When they were infants, Emma placed them safely behind the platform piano while she sang or preached or both. When they became toddlers, she was forced to leave them with her mother and sister anytime she and Allie left home to conduct a revival meeting. As the children grew into school age, a competent housekeeper maintained the home during the parents' long travel absences. Although Emma never considered this an ideal arrangement, she saw no other way.

The care of her children was a constant concern to Emma, yet she was compelled to continue answering her call to preach. This made summer the happiest time for Emma and Allie, because the children were able to travel with them. Ray played the trombone, Paul the cornet, and Ruth the piano. Allie and Emma alternated at preaching and song leading, and they both sang specials. As a family they furnished the whole program, so understandably their schedule of camp meeting and local church engagements kept their summers full.

Emma and Allie's children were the joy of the Irick home. Balancing the duties of the home with the exacting demands of her call from God was not always easy for Emma or for the children she loved. This was certainly a consideration in her decision to accept a pastorate in Lufkin, Texas. Then at least one of the parents could be with the children every week.

Emma's three children eventually grew to adulthood and made choices for their lifework. Ray experienced an eye defect that prevented the fruition of his lifelong plan to become a commercial pilot. He took courses at Bethany Nazarene College in Bethany, Oklahoma, and Texas Holiness University, and he graduated from the University of Oklahoma in Norman. He established a furniture business in Lufkin and later in Houston.

Paul, a star basketball player, received an athletic scholarship and graduated from Stephen F. Austin College. He served as a coach for several years before he became a Texas Boy Scout executive. He then was asked to head the county junior probation office in Houston, later becoming supervisor of the entire adult probation division of the county.

Ruth graduated from high school in Bethany, Oklahoma, and then moved to Lufkin, Texas. She became a bookkeeper and began working in a local funeral home, later marrying its owner, Curtis Metcalf. All three children kept in close contact with their mother, but especially Ruth and her children became Emma's constant support in later years.

5
A Fruitful Field of Service

Allie and Emma began their ministry under the auspices of the Holiness Association of Texas, a loose-knit interdenominational group of believers in Bible holiness. While this organization was born in the Lone Star State, it had members in several neighboring states. Though limited in number, members did not lack vision or enthusiasm. Some members of the association belonged to the Holiness Church of Christ, a Southern denomination.

In God's timing, another group of Holiness believers came together on the West Coast of the United States at approximately the same time. Dr. P. F. Bresee, their leader, was a very successful pastor and administrator in the Methodist Episcopal Church. His desire to preach Holiness to the poor led him to an inner-city mission in downtown Los Angeles. Soon the doors of his lifelong denomination were closed to his ministry, and he launched out to establish a church that would, as he saw the issues, be true to John Wesley's doctrine and mission. The work was organized in 1895 as the Church of the Nazarene, and under God's blessing it prospered. Within the next few years, numerous other churches either were planted or joined his group, further spreading their Holiness message.

Under similar circumstances, a group of Holiness believers on the eastern shores of the United States joined together to form the Association of Pentecostal Churches of America. In 1907 the Western and the Eastern groups met in Chicago and united to form the Pentecostal Church of the Nazarene. Seven appointed representatives from the Holiness Church of Christ went to Chicago as observers. Since they were considering uniting with the newly formed denomination, they issued an invitation for another General Assembly to be held the next year (October 1908) at Pilot Point, Texas.

Dr. Bresee did not wait until that scheduled meeting to visit Texas. Evangelist "Uncle Bud" Robinson, a member of the Holiness Association of Texas, conducted a revival meeting for the Nazarenes in Los Angeles and invited Dr. Bresee to come to Texas for a revival at the university in April 1908.

After a week of dynamic preaching from the Book of Isaiah, Dr. Bresee climaxed his appeal on Sunday night with a stirring message from Isa. 60:1: "Arise, shine; for thy light is come" (KJV). Then he offered a challenge to those who wanted to become a part of organized Holiness through the Church of the Nazarene to come to the platform. Some honestly felt that they could advance the Holiness cause best by remaining with their individual denominations. Amid shouts of victory, however, 113 men and women responded and joined the fledgling denomination on that night. Among those on the platform were Emma Wyland and her soon-to-be-husband, Allie Irick.

Dr. Bresee was totally honest with these new members. He exhorted, "We have nothing but the canopy of stars to offer. It will take real soldiers to fight the good fight of faith, and to go out under the stars and hew out a kingdom."[1]

After a summer of evangelizing following their wedding, Allie and Emma Irick were among the large group that gathered as delegates to witness the official uniting of the two church groups. The marked unity of believers, the glory of the Lord upon business sessions and services, and the unified purpose of organized Holiness evangelism made this an unforgettable occasion for Allie and Emma.

It seemed fitting that Emma was ordained on September 11, 1911, by Dr. Bresee, who had received her into membership three years earlier. She had already served more than two years in active, full-time evangelism, and to her final earthly day she was true to her ordination charge from God through Dr. Bresee. Emma strongly believed that the Holy Spirit could and should be outpoured upon all Christian believers of every era of time. This was still God's method of "purifying their hearts by faith" (Acts 15:9, KJV) and building His Church in our day.

6

Bearing Fruit in Evangelism

Allie and Emma Irick entered into a tremendously fruitful era of evangelism. They established their home at Pilot Point, Texas, and traveled across the United States in effective Holiness ministry. They were especially used of God during the summers to minister in the many interdenominational Holiness camp meetings already established across the nation. They thoroughly believed that the cause of Christian holiness could best be promoted and conserved through a church group whose cardinal commitment was to the doctrine, experience, and life of Bible holiness. They gave themselves freely to build God's kingdom through their chosen denomination.

Today's evangelists are accustomed to traveling from one established church to another at the call of a pastor or a church board or both. Allie and Emma would often go to an area where only one person had invited them and stay until a church was established. They sometimes met with severe opposition to their message, including rotten eggs and vegetables. But they often stayed until their persecutors became their supporters.

One such call was to the small town of Princeton in south Florida, where a Dr. O'Bannon had gone to practice medicine. He saw the desperate spiritual needs of his people, and, with no church in the town, he took it upon himself to call on Allie and Emma to come help him. The doctor explained the difficult circumstances, and, after much prayer, Allie and Emma consented, traveling by train from Shreveport, Louisiana.

The doctor had rented a dance pavilion for two weeks, and one of the first converts was the dance hall pianist, who was the owner's daughter. She told her mother she would never play again for the dances. Emma described her part: "We fasted, prayed, preached, sang, and shouted."[1] God was faithful, and before they left town, a church was organized—a church that not only remains today but also is one of the largest evangelical establishments in southern Florida.

On another occasion, Allie and Emma had just finished the Alabama State Camp Meeting at Nauvoo, Alabama, when the superintendent of a large coal mine implored them to come to his mining camp for four days of meetings. The couple had four free days before their next scheduled meeting, so they agreed to go with their new friend, feeling strongly that God was involved in this invitation.

On the final day of that fruitful campaign in the coal camp community building, the mine superintendent begged them to go down into the mine with him and preach to the many men who had not attended the meetings. A mile and a half underground and one mile from the shaft, a pile of rocks had been erected for a pulpit and a rough plank erected in the muddy floor for an altar. Allie sang, prayed, and played the portable organ before Emma preached and gave an altar call. Five miners knelt in the mud and prayed through. One of these five was the mine superintendent's father, a 65-year-old man who had never before sought God publicly.

Three years later, that same mine superintendent contacted the Iricks to tell them that his father had recently died, but not without leaving a message for Allie and Emma Irick: "Tell them that if they had not come down into the mine I would never have made it. I'll meet them in heaven."[2]

In another meeting the altar was filled with seekers who became happy finders. Their singing and praise to God antagonized several neighbors, who persuaded the local sheriff to stop the revival. That officer walked up the center aisle and announced that the meeting was canceled by court order. Emma rose to the occasion. She called out to him, "Let me pray about this first," and without waiting for the officer's approval, she began. When she had finished praying, the sheriff was gone, and they never saw him again.

In 1920 Allie and Emma's deep interest in home missions carried them into a new responsibility as superintendent of the church district in west Texas. During this six-year span of their ministry, they planted an average of six churches each year. They used a large tent to enter new communities and organized a congregation whenever 10 adults committed themselves to support the baby church. Several of the largest present-day Nazarene churches in Texas were started in this manner.

The Iricks faced many unusual difficulties in their church planting endeavors. Their 1925 Christmas vacation, for example, was spent in Lamesa, Texas. They took their children along and stayed an extra week. Emma taught the children their lessons, a task with which she was thoroughly familiar. The meeting was held in a tent, using gasoline torches for light and heat.

In the middle of the campaign, as Emma vividly remembered it, "a blue 'norther' with hard winds blew through that little town and split the tent completely in two." What did she do? "We did the only thing we could do," she related. "I sewed on that tent all day, from eight o'clock in the morning until five o'clock that night. I felt like the Apostle Paul, who was a tentmaker. We held services and God honored our hard work with an altar full of seekers on that freezing night."[3]

Also during this time of ministry, along with her work in home missions, Emma frequently served as interim pastor of a church in Pilot Point, Texas, where they maintained their home. She also helped support the family with her efforts on their small farm; the garden was especially beneficial.

In carrying out some of her duties as interim pastor, Emma became associated with an enterprise that held her prayerful interest the rest of her life. Two of Allie's close friends and preaching associates were John and Ed Roberts. Another brother had established Rest Cottage, a home for unwed mothers at Pilot Point. Emma's heart was strongly drawn to the plight and spiritual needs of these young girls. She encouraged them not only to give their lives to Christ but also to love their babies enough to consider allowing their adoption by parents who would give them a Christian home. Later in her evangelistic and pastoral ministry, Emma raised offerings to support Rest Cottage. In all of this she was spiritually caring and consistent.

In 1926 the Iricks resigned their responsibilities in Texas and moved to Bethany, Oklahoma, to enable the boys to enter college and Ruth to attend high school. Allie and Emma reentered the field of nationwide evangelism. For the next seven years they traveled the United States, doing what they loved best—preaching the gospel of full salvation wherever doors of opportunity opened.

7
The Fruit of Pastoral Ministry

In 1933 Allie and Emma were at the peak of their career in evangelism. The couple had become well known across the nation and were especially in demand for dozens of independent and denominational Holiness camps during this strong camp meeting era. They had a full slate of scheduled revivals for the next three years. They owned a home in Bethany, Oklahoma. Professionally, the Iricks had it made.

Then Emma received a letter from Lufkin, Texas, that was to change the direction of all her future life and ministry. Across the years Allie and Emma had conducted three revival campaigns in this small town in southeastern Texas. They had always been well received by the church and community. Now, however, this church in Lufkin was experiencing extremely hard times. The congregation had been without a pastor for several months. Attendance had dwindled. In the heart of the depression that was gripping the nation, finances were at an all-time low, with only two men from the congregation able to find work. Several prospective pastors had turned down the invitation to come as their human leader.

Finally, after a prolonged intercessory prayer meeting, someone suggested that they ask Emma Irick to be their pastor. As this board member expressed, "I know she will say 'Yes' if God leads her to answer our call."[1] The church board unanimously and enthusiastically agreed, and the letter was mailed.

As in every decision Emma made, she took the call seriously and fasted and prayed until God's answer came. Clearly and unmistakably, Emma then knew that God wanted her to become the pastor of the church in Lufkin. But her problem was not settled, for Allie had no similar inclination to make such a drastic change of direction in ministry. They had been married for 25 years, and up to now they had been in total agreement concerning the direction God wanted them to take.

Emma had obeyed the Lord as a 14-year-old girl when she sought God for salvation. She was equally as obedient when she was entirely sanctified and when she accepted God's call to become a preacher of the glorious gospel of Christ. She had prayed through about her marriage choice. Emma and Allie had always sought God's guidance—even to the point of agreeing about their evangelistic calls and challenges. Emma was totally convinced that God was leading her in this new direction.

Allie finally agreed to move with Emma to Lufkin. She could become the pastor, and he would continue their revival slate, in order to be fair to the churches and leaders where they were already scheduled. Emma and Allie packed their furniture and belongings into a moving van. They left Bethany, Oklahoma, on a Saturday morning with their two younger children. After stopping to preach at Pilot Point, Texas, on Sunday, they decided to start out after the evening service and drive on to Lufkin. They arrived early on that Labor Day morning.

The Iricks' first view of the church and nearby parsonage was depressing. The rutted, weed-grown yard of the church, Emma felt, was a public disgrace. To the children, Lufkin seemed to be "the jumping-off place." They both said, "Let's turn around and go back." Emma, though distressed, was not discouraged. She told them, "It doesn't always have to be this way."

After two days of cleaning out the deteriorated parsonage, the family moved in. Allie immediately left town for his revival schedule in western Texas, and their son returned to Oklahoma. Then Emma rallied the only available help, several women of the church, to change the disgraceful appearance of the churchyard. She borrowed a wagon and a mule. She and these ladies made several trips across town to the riverbank, where they hand shoveled loads of rich topsoil.

The sight of the new pastor driving that mule was the best possible community advertisement that the church was under new management. Before Sunday arrived, the townspeople—and especially the grateful neighbors—were amazed to see the flowers, shrubs, and terraced topsoil planted with grass. They soon began to call it "the church with the park around it."

Only 21 people were in Sunday School that first Sunday, with 31 present for the preaching service. They gave their hardworking new pastor an offering of $2.55 for her week's work.

One week later, a heavy weekend rain demonstrated that the parsonage roof leaked. On Monday morning Emma entered the attic and poked sticks and nails through the gaping holes in the roof. Then she purchased a bundle of shingles, mounted a ladder, and proceeded to repair the roof. Her philosophy was the old adage "God helps those who help themselves."

Later that week she went to the bank, which was threatening foreclosure for $900 owed by the church on a new street assessment. The bank president, who had seen her on the roof, not only extended the necessary credit but also contributed $100 for the project. Emma cried for joy at this evidence that God was working to build His church and meet their needs.

Allie called Prof. John E. Moore, a well-known singer of that day, to come for a hastily scheduled fall revival campaign. Allie arrived home in time to preach, along with Emma, for that two-week revival spanning three Sundays (a normal schedule in that day). New people were reached, and the church was inspired to believe for greater days ahead. It was an auspicious beginning for what was to become 26 years of Emma's faithful, fruitful service to God and that Lufkin church.

The providential leading in Emma's drastic life change from evangelist to pastor became completely evident when, just three and a half months after moving to Lufkin, Allie was stricken with a debilitating stroke while conducting a revival in Riverside, California. When he was able to return home, he needed constant care. Had Emma still been an evangelist, her ministry would have largely ended, since she could not have left him alone. Now, however, she was able to give him the needed care while still carrying on her pastoral ministry.

The next 15 years were difficult ones for

Emma. Allie recovered very slowly from the effects of his stroke, and he required constant attention and support. Emma massaged the paralyzed muscles on his right side hundreds of times in those first 2 years. By that time he was able to move about in a wheelchair.

Added to this nursing duty were the normal household chores of cooking and cleaning, as well as the challenge of preparing three sermons every week. As Emma became better known in the community, calls for her pastoral services increased. She insisted that any member or friend of the local church should have a pastoral call and prayer before and following any surgery or hospital stay. At all hours of the day or night, calls came to the parsonage about some sick or needy person or family. Emma would immediately go and minister, whether or not she had previously met them. For the entire community she became *the* pastor to call in Lufkin in any time of need.

Emma's old friend from her days at Peniel, "Uncle Buddy" Robinson, paid a preaching visit to Lufkin in 1937. He reported his impressions in his "Good Samaritan

Chat" in the *Herald of Holiness*. Among other things, Uncle Bud was impressed with the terrific biscuits and rabbit dinner Emma served him. His report on the local church and pastor was a great tribute to her ministry: "She has more things in her favor than almost any woman you'll meet in a year's travel. She is a great preacher, a great cook, and a splendid housekeeper." What Uncle Buddy saw in Lufkin encouraged him to add, "If we will keep clean, humble, on fire, and with a vision, victory will continue to be ours."[2]

Emma was often asked for her biscuit recipe. She always mixed her biscuits right in the top of the flour sack, avoiding the mess flour makes when this operation is moved to a table or countertop. She had learned this method while still a child cook and housekeeper at her parents' home in Kansas. Whether or not this was the secret of those melt-in-your-mouth creations, her biscuits always drew rave reviews from every guest at her table.

After several years, Allie showed enough improvement to be able to preach occasionally, though always with difficulty. Like Emma, his preaching always majored on the doctrine, experience, and life of holiness. Speaking from his wheelchair, he was still "able to speak with forcefulness when moved by the Holy Spirit."[3] He became a living testimony to their congregation that God's grace was sufficient for every situation faced in life. Emma's tribute to his preaching was: "He could feed my soul more than any preacher I ever heard." She further testified, "The deep faith and spiritual insight he possessed were revealed in his everyday life as a husband, a father, and a servant of God."[4]

God's promise to Emma when she was called to preach was amply fulfilled during her pastoral years. Under her ministry, several men from the local church were called to preach and are still fulfilling that call. She also saw others under her influence become missionaries for Christ in foreign lands. "God always keeps His word"[5] was Emma's humble explanation for these miracles of grace.

Allie's last months on earth were filled with much suffering. In one of his last lucid moments he said, "Mother, continue to carry on. Do all you can on your own, and then please do a little extra for me."[6] Emma later testified that she and Allie frequently prayed together as Allie neared the end of life. On December 28, 1948, Allie was called to his eternal reward. Dr. V. H. Lewis, his district superintendent, conducted the funeral service for this pioneer preacher-evangelist.

Emma continued to "carry on," as her late husband had exhorted her to do. God prospered the church in Lufkin, and attendance eventually reached a high of 442. Beginning in November 1952, the congregation focused their attention upon the desperate need of a new building to house their growing church and Sunday School congregation. For 22 months Emma raised a special offering every week. Services were conducted in the Lufkin Community Building while the old church was torn down and a beautiful new edifice erected. Characteristically, Emma led the ladies of her church in many days and months of physical labor during these years. Her example challenged the men of her congregation and community to donate their time, energy, and skills to the project.

Several evidences of God's provision became apparent during this building program. Once, when all funds were exhausted, an unsolicited letter arrived from a friend in Mississippi, reading, "I had been saving this for my burial, but God told me to send it to you, Sister Irick, to help on that church."[7] In another emergency, Emma was strongly impressed to sell her own retirement home in Bethany and give the entire amount to help finish the church. Such Spirit-led generosity challenged others in sacrificial giving, and the project was completed.

8

Choice Fruit in Old Age

In 1959 Emma felt a holy restlessness about her ministry in Lufkin. She had pastored the church for 26 years following her 25 years as a traveling evangelist. She was now 71 years of age and still in remarkably good health. Most preachers, men or women, would have looked forward to a well-earned retirement.

But not Emma Irick! Her sense of release from her pastoral responsibility was God's signal to her that she faced yet another challenge. Increasingly she was convinced that she should go back on the road again as a traveling evangelist. Calls from several districts for home mission tours confirmed these inner spiritual impressions.

It was not easy to leave the pastorate in Lufkin. As she described her feelings, "I had to beg the Lord to take at least part of my love for my church family out of my heart, for it was like giving up my own children."[1]

Her resignation was just as difficult for her beloved Lufkin people. In a farewell "Emma Irick, This Is Your Life" service, the people extolled her faithful ministry to them. The service concluded with this farewell statement: "It is with many regrets, heartaches, and disappointments that now, after 26 years of your ministry, filled with unselfish love and devotion to each of us, the inevitable has come. The vastness of your experience, depth of soul burden, and magnanimity of spirit and mind have demanded freedom from any locality. God and the general church beckon. Surely the world is now your parish."[2]

The congregation petitioned Emma to continue to maintain her home in Lufkin as a haven whenever her new evangelism schedule made this possible. In early October 1959, she embarked on her new career, beginning with a mission tour in the Philadelphia area. In the years ahead she toured throughout the United States. She was especially used of God in preaching to preachers. Her constant challenge to them was to "get the sand out of your socks"[3] and preach second-blessing holiness of heart and life. Through these contacts, she received many calls to come to local churches for revival campaigns. Soon her evangelistic slate was filled for months and even years ahead.

In 1958, a year before she resigned her pastorate in Lufkin, Emma was the featured speaker at the golden anniversary celebration of the denomination she had joined 50 years earlier under Dr. Phineas F. Bresee. Again the gathering was held in a large tent in Pilot Point, Texas, representative of that significant 1908 event in which Emma participated. All who attended this historic occasion will never forget her electrifying challenge to be true to the purposes for which God had raised up this denomination. She already had completed 50 years of continuous preaching ministry. That record would have been enough for most preachers, but not for Emma Irick. She went on amazingly for 20 more years of pastoral and nationwide evangelistic ministry.

In 1964 she preached for one unforgettable week at Nazarene Theological Seminary in Kansas City. One of her most significant sermons there was an exposition of
John 14:16. She challenged the student
preachers to be like Jesus and always tailor
their message to each congregation. In con-
clusion, she challenged them, as Dr. Bresee
had challenged her, to "go out . . . and hew
out a kingdom."

In 1973 Nazarene Publishing House pub-
lished Emma's autobiography, *The King's
Daughter.* This testimonial booklet included
various tributes from her local church and
district leaders. She wrote her story "with a
prayer that it will be an inspiration to the
present generation of the church, both young
and old, to love and serve God in the beauty
of holiness."[4]

Emma was always fiercely independent,
determined to care for herself and never to be
confined to a group retirement home. In
1968 she was able to buy a small house in
Lufkin. Her daughter, Ruth, desired to be
near her beloved mother, who was now 80
years of age, and built her own house across

the street from her mother's little brick home. Emma cherished this loving daily concern and care exhibited by her daughter and grandchildren, while they still allowed her to direct her own lifestyle. She made Ruth promise never to confine her to a nursing home, something Emma passionately dreaded.

Emma had been emotionally prepared, as much as is humanly possible, when her husband died in 1948 after his long illness. She was not prepared, however, for the death of her sons, Ray in 1958 and Paul in 1973. Again she proved to her family and friends that God's grace is sufficient in every sorrow that comes our way.

In 1975 Emma underwent hip replacement surgery. Her family used this opportunity to retire her treasured automobile, and thereafter all of her travel was done by train, plane, or a car chauffeured by someone from her personal or church family.

In 1978 Emma finally officially retired. She was now 90 years of age and still in remarkably good health. She had completed 70 years of continuous and effective ministry. Although she gave up her cross-country ministry schedule, she still accepted preaching invitations from churches in her immediate area. She especially enjoyed teaching an appreciative Sunday School class every week she was at home in Lufkin.

In October 1983 Emma was asked to be a featured speaker at the 75th anniversary celebration of the organization of the Church of the Nazarene. The ceremony was held again in a tent at Pilot Point, Texas. By this time Emma was the only surviving Nazarene elder who had been present at that celebrated meeting in 1908. She preached from her wheelchair because of recent surgery, but she had lost none of her famous dynamic.

Emma had begun her ministry without the aid of any of the electronic equipment that helps modern speakers protect their voices. Especially in camp meetings, in all kinds of weather, she had preached to hundreds of people without any artificial voice amplification. She praised God that she had been able to preach those thousands of sermons in her lifetime without even a hint of laryngitis.

The *Lufkin Daily News* interviewed Emma in 1984 on her 96th birthday. The reporter found her still "a very happy person, who was still living in her best days. She reads two newspapers and watches four TV newscasts every day. She spends an hour writing letters, and three hours in reading and devotions." The impact of aging on her active lifestyle did "bother her some." Her testimony was that "it's been a great life, a wonderful life, and a full life." The reporter recorded that she still "had the memory of an elephant, and a heart just as big."[5]

In a videotaped interview with Dr. V. H. Lewis, Emma rejoiced that though she could no longer fill the pulpit, she had now become a prayer warrior. She prayed every day for her church leaders as well as for the many people who wrote asking to be remembered in her "effectual fervent prayer[s]" (James 5:16, KJV). This intercession became the labor and joy of her last days on earth.

In August 1984 Emma suffered a stroke at her home in Lufkin. When she was released from the hospital a month later, her doctor ordered her to be placed in a nursing home. Her daughter, Ruth, reluctantly agreed. Since no room was yet available at a chosen new facility in Lufkin, Emma was moved to a nursing home in Wells, Texas, 20 miles north of her home. Emma learned that her fears of such confinement were groundless. A month later, when space became available in Lufkin, Emma did not want to leave Wells. She had been treated so well and had found such joy in witnessing to new friends and caregivers that she loved her new home. She agreed to the transfer only because it would be easier for her daughter and grandchildren to visit her daily if she moved back to Lufkin.

Emma's stroke made it impossible for her to read or hold her Bible, which she had read regularly from cover to cover for many years. During those difficult months she enjoyed her tape player and Dr. Earl Lee's services and sermons from Pasadena, California, First Church of the Nazarene.

Emma died on December 31, 1984, just a few days before her 97th birthday. Dr. V. H. Lewis, who had preached her husband's funeral 36 years earlier, led her family and the Lufkin church, along with representatives and friends from across the nation, in a victorious memorial tribute. The cold weather and a howling snowstorm could not detract from the victorious memorial celebration of this veteran soldier of the Cross. She is buried beside her husband and near her two sons in the Lufkin cemetery, awaiting God's final trumpet call and her bodily resurrection.

Emma lived her life and preached to others in the assurance of life eternal through faith in our resurrected Christ. She never hesitated to preach that there was a devil's hell to shun and a heaven to gain. She stayed true to her heritage of faith to the very end of her earthly pilgrimage. This preaching mother never deviated from her divine calling. She turned many to righteousness. She certainly qualifies, as described by the prophet Daniel, to join that select group of saints who will "shine . . . like the stars for ever and ever" (Dan. 12:3).

Emma loved the cause of organized Holiness and put her all into the Kingdom. She was "grateful to have lived in the pioneer period of her church's history, and to have had a little part in this glorious work."[6] To this veteran, her church was "a great stream of salvation flowing on like a mighty Mississippi River."[7]

From the vantage point of her personal "romance of faith," the future of the church "looks glorious." Her admonition was that "if we will keep clean, humble, on fire, and with a vision, victory will continue to be ours. May God bless our Beloved Zion, is my daily prayer."[8]

Notes

Chapter 1

1. Emma Irick, *The King's Daughter* (Kansas City: Pedestal Press, 1973), 13.

Chapter 2

1. Irick, *The King's Daughter,* 19.

2. Ibid., 15-16.

3. Ellen Temple, "Rev. Emma Irick: A Blessing to Everyone," *Lufkin (Tex.) Free Press,* January 19, 1978.

4. Irick, *The King's Daughter,* 16.

5. Ibid.

6. Emma Irick, interview by J. Kenneth Grider, Lufkin, Tex., March 18, 1964, reel-to-reel audio recording. On file at Nazarene Archives, Kansas City.

7. Ibid.

8. Irick, *The King's Daughter,* 20.

9. Ibid.

10. Ibid., 44.

Chapter 3

1. Irick, *The King's Daughter,* 20.

2. Emma Irick, chapel service sermon, Nazarene Theological Seminary, December 2, 1964, reel-to-reel audio recording. On file at Nazarene Archives, Kansas City.

3. Ibid.

Chapter 4

1. Irick, *The King's Daughter,* 17.

2. Ibid., 22.

Chapter 5

1. Irick, *The King's Daughter,* 29.

Chapter 6
1. Emma Irick, *Early History of the Church of the Nazarene,* March 15, 1956, reel-to-reel audio recording. On file at Nazarene Archives, Kansas City.

2. Irick, *The King's Daughter,* 52.

3. Ibid., 52-53.

Chapter 7
1. Emma Irick, interview by Arlita Hallam, Lufkin, Tex., August 30, 1980, set of two audiocassettes. On file at Nazarene Archives, Kansas City.

2. Bud Robinson, "Good Samaritan Chat," *Herald of Holiness,* April 10, 1937, 12.

3. James McGraw, "The Preaching of Allie Irick," *Preacher's Magazine,* January 1958, 8.

4. Irick, *The King's Daughter,* 62.

5. Ibid., 20.

6. Ibid., 62.

7. Ibid., 60.

Chapter 8
1. Emma Irick, chapel service sermon, Nazarene Theological Seminary, December 4, 1964, reel-to-reel audio recording. On file at Nazarene Archives, Kansas City.

2. "Rev. Emma Irick: A Blessing to Everyone."

3. McGraw, "The Preaching of Allie Irick," 10.

4. Irick, *The King's Daughter,* 6.

5. Dan Hill, "Her Legacy Will Live On," *Lufkin (Tex.) Daily News,* January 1, 1985.

6. Irick, *The King's Daughter,* 22.

7. Emma Irick, chapel service sermon, Nazarene Theological Seminary, December 1, 1964, reel-to-reel audio recording. On file at Nazarene Archives, Kansas City.

8. Irick, *The King's Daughter,* 44.

Bibliography

Books

Irick, Allie and Emma. *A Journey 'Round the World.*
Louisville, Ky.: Pentecostal Publishing Co., 1907.

Irick, Emma. *The King's Daughter.* Kansas City: Pedestal
Press, 1973.

Articles

Hill, Dan. "Her Legacy Will Live On." *Lufkin (Tex.) Daily
News,* January 1, 1985.

McGraw, James. "The Preaching of Allie Irick." *Preacher's
Magazine,* January 1958.

Robinson, Bud. "Good Samaritan Chat." *Herald of Holiness,*
April 10, 1937, 12.

Temple, Ellen. "Rev. Emma Irick: A Blessing to Everyone."
Lufkin (Tex.) Free Press, January 19, 1978.

Video Recording

Irick, Emma. Interview by Dr. V. H. Lewis, Pilot Point, Tex.,
1983. Series of five videotapes. On file at Nazarene
Archives, Kansas City.

Sound Recordings

Irick, Emma. *Early History of the Church of the Nazarene,*
March 15, 1956. Reel-to-reel audio recording. On file at
Nazarene Archives, Kansas City.

————. Chapel service sermons, Nazarene Theological Seminary, December 1, 2, 4, 1964. Reel-to-reel audio record-
ings. On file at Nazarene Archives, Kansas City.

————. Interview by J. Kenneth Grider, Lufkin, Tex., March
18, 1964. Reel-to-reel audio recording. On file at Nazarene Archives, Kansas City.

————. Interview by Arlita Hallam, Lufkin, Tex., August 30,
1980. Set of two audiocassettes. On file at Nazarene
Archives, Kansas City.

———. Excerpts of preaching. Audiocassette. Used at the Church of the Nazarene General Assembly evangelism exhibit, 1980. On file at Nazarene Archives, Kansas City.